Sixty and Better!

*Making the Most of the
Golden Years*

Joe McKeever

Bertha Fagan McKeever

&

Parson's Porch Books

www.parsonsporchbooks.com

Sixty and Better!: Making the Most of the Golden Years

ISBN: Softcover 978-1-946478-92-4

Sixty and Better!

Contents

Dedication

We dedicate this book to our wonderful siblings, all of whom meet the qualifications for seniorhood (and sainthood, too!) and do it with class and honor:

Ronald J. McKeever - Ron, the patriarch of our family these days, preaches three times a week as pastor of Mount Pisgah Baptist Church outside Birmingham, Alabama

Laura Pepper Sharp - Laura teaches Sunday School at her UMC church and works full-time running the office at an automobile auction

Patricia McKeever Phelps - Patricia, the best cook in North Alabama, spends her days helping to raise some wonderful great-granddaughters

Carolyn McKeever Lampman - Carolyn, treasurer of her UMC church, is the full-time care-giver for Van, her husband of nearly 30 years

Preface

They say that tightrope walkers are most susceptible to accidents when they are almost finished and nearly "home." They've been on stage and risked their lives; they've done well. Now, it's time to take their bow and call it a day. But as they approach the end, they have to watch their last steps. One slip and life comes crashing down.

Think of that as a metaphor for life. Even after doing well for many years, it's still possible to undo all the good we have done by becoming careless at the end.

That's the burden of our little book. Consider it a reminder to stay faithful.

A note of explanation: In the chapters which follow both Bertha and Joe had input, but the voice you will be "hearing" is mostly Joe. Sometimes, when it's necessary we identify who is speaking, but usually we don't because it doesn't matter.

Introduction

I was sitting at home in front of the television one night. The phone rang. A voice said, "Sir, I'm conducting a survey of people's television-watching habits. It'll only take three minutes." I said, "Go ahead."

"First," he said, "What group are you in: 25 and under. 25 to 35. 35 to 45. 45 to 55. Or, 55 and up?"

I said, "That one."

He said, "Which one?"

I said, "55 and up."

Click.

He was gone.

It felt like the perfect illustration of the value our culture places on the older generation. You're old? You don't count. You're a senior? Leave the game. You're elderly? Is there someone else available?

But 55? Yikes. My oldest child Neil is that age. If he's over the hill, what does that make me, his dad?

Our culture wants to take the most seasoned veterans in the room and mute them. To disarm the warriors who have fought life's battles and stood the test of the years.

Not real smart.

Fortunately, you and I do not ask the world what role it wants us to play. We do not get our self-esteem from a poll or survey. We do not go up and down the street and question our neighbors on whether we should have a voice in today's world.

We were created in the image of God. We were redeemed by the Lord Jesus Christ. We are more than conquerors through Him who loved us.

And none of that is up for a vote, friend.

Garson Kanin's *It Takes a Long Time to Become Young*-- which I read years ago and was never able to forget-- was prompted by his alarm at how older people were being treated by businesses, lawmakers, and society as a whole. And, while we agree with his concern and applaud efforts to end what is called "ageism," that is not the thrust of our little volume.

What concerns us--and hopefully bothers our readers--is seeing a lot of older people do that very thing to themselves. They marginalize themselves because they are getting up in years. They dismiss their importance because they've managed to hang on (and hang around) longer than many of their peers.

Think of the irony of that. They've been successful in living and working and holding on and as a result they lose their self-esteem? They conclude they no longer matter because they won the lottery?

Not real smart.

We all know people in their 50s, 60s, and beyond, who feel that since society wants to push them off the stage, somehow, they have surrendered all rights to a decent self-respect and a good life.

"I don't count; I'm old," you'll hear them say.

Listen to their conversation. "I'm older than dirt," one said the other day. Another said, "My granddaughter asked me, 'Mimi, are you a hundred?'" The problem is that Mimi internalizes that and comes away feeling ancient instead of treasuring what should have been a precious moment.

Recently, I was at Fort Bragg to speak at a prayer breakfast. The night before, Chaplain Wayne Scholle and his wife Lara took me to dinner with their children. At the end of the evening as we were saying our good-nights, the youngest child, five-year-old Elizabeth--as cute as God ever made any child--said to me, "Mister Joe. You...you....you are almost dead!" We had a good laugh. I gave her a hug and said, "Honey, I'm closer than I've ever been. But I'm not there yet."

Suppose I had taken that child's sweet little comment to heart! Imagine me growing despondent from something a child said. After all, to a five-year-old, seventy years and seven hundred years are pretty much the same.

So...

We'd like to say a few things to those of us who are moving into the stratosphere of life, piling up those big birthday numbers, setting new family records for longevity!

Congratulations! You are a winner.

Count yourself blessed! Not everyone makes it to this age. Do yourself a favor and stop giving it such a negative spin. It's perfectly fine to be 60. Or 70. 80, 90, whatever.

Look around at your classmates. Many of them were not so blessed as you.

Seize that age. Make the most of it. You're younger than you will ever be again.

And hey-- if it's this much fun being 78 (our age at the moment), imagine what the 80s are going to be like!

Okay now...

Much of what follows is light-hearted and intended as fun. We even dropped in some of my cartoons we thought you'd enjoy. (Use them if you can. Print them out and turn them into place mats at your next senior luncheon. Use them on posters. To see a few thousand of my toons, go to the website for Baptist Press www.bpnews.net and click on 'comics.')

We--Bertha and Joe--are having the time of our lives right now. So, we don't intend this book as a scholarly dissertation, but something from our hearts to yours.

We hope it encourages you. If so, don't let the book gather dust on a shelf, but pass it along after you've read it.

My friend Bruce Fields, in his 60s now (and probably more youthful than at any time in his life) does that. Over in Gainesville, Georgia, where he is on staff at the First Baptist Church, when he finishes a book, rather than add it to an already huge collection, Bruce looks around for someone who would enjoy it, and passes it on. They're impressed, he does a good turn, and life goes forward.

Chapter One

"Let's make these the best years of our lives!"

"It's not how old you are; it's how you're old." --Groucho Marx

Groucho was half right. How old we are does matter for a lot of reasons. But how we handle our (ahem) advanced age is just as important. So, let's give Groucho credit for being clever and almost right.

Now, I don't want to get ridiculous about it. I'm not exactly in favor of creaking bones and loose teeth, of age spots, stooped shoulders, shortness of breath or dementia. And yet...

There is so much to be said for these latter years of our earthly existence. We are having the time of our lives. At the moment, we're both 78 years old. Widowed after 52 years of marriage--Bertha to Dr. Gary Fagan and Joe to Margaret Henderson--we met and married and bought a house in a lovely neighborhood and merged our furniture. We joined a local church and began meeting our neighbors. We're loving life.

One of my favorite things is addressing senior groups. So far this year, I have spoken to seniors in the Mississippi cities of Canton, Summit, Hattiesburg, Clinton, Long Beach, Wiggins, Wynndale, Poplarville, Leakesville, and Philadelphia; in Texas at Alto Frio Campgrounds and Jacksonville; in Louisiana at Lake Providence; and in Alabama at Tuscumbia. Before the year is out, I'll be addressing seniors in York, Alabama, Columbus, MS, and Atlanta, GA.

Often when addressing seniors in churches, I'll begin like this...

"Good morning! I've driven up from Jackson, Mississippi, to congratulate you on the two greatest blessings of your life! Number one, you're saved. You've been forgiven of your sins, you're a child of the King, the Lord Jesus Christ has received you into His forever family, you are going to Heaven! And number two...

You're old.

They laugh. I pause, then say: *Most of us in this room can remember friends who would have given all they own to have lived as long as we have lived. To have seen their children grow to be adults, to have been there when they married, to have held their grandbabies in their arms. And some of us have had the privilege of seeing our grandchildren become adults. Of my eight grandchildren, at this moment all but one are in their 20s. I am blessed. And so are you."*

Later in the message, I'll say a special word to those seniors who love to gripe and complain. We've all met them!

"Now, if you want to feel bad and worry about the future, there are actually reasons to do so. In fact, I'll give you four. Number one, you're old. Number two, you're getting older. (They're smiling by now. They know I'm putting them on.) Number three, you're going to die. And number four, chances are before you die you will have a lot of medical problems and medical bills.

So, if you want to worry and feel bad about the future, get on with it. There are very real reasons to do so."

I pause to let that sink in, then continue...

However, most of us do not want to feel bad and worry about the future. We'd rather rejoice and be thankful. So, if that's you-- if you want to rejoice, Christian, I have good news for you: There are ten thousand reasons to do so....

--We are saved, born again, washed in the blood of the Lamb, adopted into the family of God. We are new creatures, old things have passed away, all things have become new!

--Our sins are gone, they're underneath the blood of the cross of Jesus Christ, as far removed as darkness is from dawn. In the sea of God's forgetfulness. Furthermore, there is no condemnation to those who are in Christ Jesus!

--God is alive, Jesus Christ is on the throne, and the Holy Spirit is with you. He indwells you, overshadows you, goes before you, comes behind you, undergirds you, and has promised never to leave nor forsake you!

--God has given you the Holy Bible to guide you, a church family to nurture you, instructions on how to serve Him in this life, and promises that are out of this world.

--God has given us work to do in this world and promised us that greater works than He did shall we do too!

--He has promised to prepare a place for us, a kingdom prepared from the foundation of the world. It is the Father's house, an inheritance incorruptible, undefiled, that fades not

away, reserved in Heaven for you, and you are kept by the power of God unto salvation ready to be revealed at the last time!

Why aren't you rejoicing?? So much to rejoice about.

Okay, slow down here...

We're not rejoicing because we're getting old. Or older.

We're not rejoicing because our hair is turning grey (or loose). We are not rejoicing because of infirmities and such, but rejoicing because He is faithful in the midst of whatever circumstances we find ourselves in.

We are people of faith in the living God. We rejoice regardless of how we are feeling today or what the doctor is saying about us or the condition of our bank account. We have far greater reasons to rejoice than we've ever had in our lives!

We rejoice because we have lived a long time, have loved a great many years, and have had time to see God do a thousand wonderful things. We rejoice because He is still at work in us and showing us delights we would never have recognized in our youth. And you can believe we rejoice because we are nearer than ever to the celestial blessings the Lord Jesus promised us.

We're rejoicing because we've had the privilege of seeing our children become middle-aged and seeing most of our grands enter their 20s. Both our spouses of 52 years, Gary and Margaret, were denied this privilege, so you might say we're doing double duty and enjoying it for them.

Remember that time when the disciples awakened the sleeping Lord Jesus in the boat? (It's in Mark 4.) "Master, the storm is swamping the boat! We're sinking! Wake up and do something." Jesus awakened and stood up. Then, looking out at the storm He proceeded to rebuke the winds, rebuke the waves, and rebuke the disciples.

"Why did you fear?" He asked. "Where is your faith?"

What a great question. Two questions, in fact. Why did we fear? Where was our faith?

I've sometimes imagined that when we stand before Him at Judgment, the Lord might point out some of those critical moments of decision-making in our lives and then, to our everlasting embarrassment, ask: "What were you afraid of? Where was your faith?"

So, as you and I go forward--as the years accumulate and the birthdays pile up and threaten to get out of hand--let us not be afraid. The news ahead is all good, friend.

We are playing with house money. (Ask your brother-in-law what that means!)

The good news from Heaven is...

In Jesus Christ, we can't lose. We are born again, a member of God's family, and destined for Heaven. To all believers, Scripture says, "There is therefore now no condemnation to those who are in Christ" (Romans 8:1). No condemnation. Imagine that. Our hearts may condemn us, and frequently do. Our memories work overtime to remind us of past failures and wrong deeds. But even if our hearts condemn us, even when we falter, our Lord remains faithful. Scripture actually says that (see 2 Timothy 2:13 and I John 3:20ff).

The question is how will we handle the future?

Suppose you are only middle-aged and wonder how you will handle the so-called golden years of life. Will you be cranky and negative? Always "agin" change and speaking of the good old days?

Actually, you and I are laying down clues all the time as to how we will handle the future. Consider this....

I used to wonder about the time when the Lord Jesus was walking the hills of Galilee, teaching the crowds and healing the sick. What would I have done had I been alive back then, I wondered. Would I have been among His devoted followers? Would I have ignored Jesus and gone on about my business? Or would I have joined the throngs yelling, "Crucify Him! Crucify Him!"

I think it's possible to know the answer to that.

I would have done then exactly as I'm doing now.

If I'm ignoring Him now, I'd have done that in the First Century. If I'm opposing Him now and criticizing Christians and scoffing at the Scriptures, I'd have done the same thing then. But if I'm among the faithful now, loving and serving Him, sitting at His feet and taking in His word, I'd have been the same way 2,000 years ago.

The same principle applies to the business of growing old, I'm thinking.

If I am serving the Lord and praising Him and being faithful in my younger, healthier years, then it's a fair bet that when I get older, I'll do the same. The best clue on how I will handle infirmity is how I'm dealing with life now, right this minute.

If I'm happily married now--and I am--and loving my spouse and friends when all is well, then it's a safe bet that I'll feel the same way if and when the life processes begin to close down, and I become resident in the nursing home or become homebound.

If I'm being faithful with my finances now, honoring God and blessing others, then I expect to be able to do that in my last years on the planet.

The best indicator of how I would handle poverty is the way I'm dealing with the money I have now.

The best indicator of how I would handle my days and nights in a nursing home is how I'm doing now in my comfortable middle-class home.

We all make choices every day. Our circumstances change, and the choices vary from day to day. How we choose to live today tells volumes about how we'll do tomorrow.

I choose to rejoice. "As for me and my house, we will serve the Lord."

I'm not passively going into the future. I'm actively serving the Lord and loving this life and the people in it.

So! If we can help a few others to do the same thing, we will count that a great privilege. Someone whom we will never meet this side of Heaven may find something helpful in this little volume. And wouldn't that be wonderful!

That's our prayer.

One summer while Jack Hinton was pastoring a church in New Bern, NC, he took a team on a mission trip to the little island nation of Tabago in the Caribbean. One day, the missionary who was their host brought them to visit a leprosarium. As the Carolina group spread out over the grounds and visited with patients, they had their hearts broken by seeing up close what leprosy does to the human body. After a bit, the administrator invited Jack to bring his team into the chapel and lead a worship service. The Carolinians lined across the front as the patients entered. Most were able to walk in under their own power; a few were helping each other. Then Pastor Jack saw something strange.

One of the women patients entered and sat on the back row, then turned to face the back wall. "What's that all about?" Jack wondered.

The group led some songs and prayers, read Scriptures and had testimonies. Finally, Pastor Jack said, "Folks, we have time for one more hymn. Does anyone have a favorite you'd like us to sing?" Now, for the first time the little woman on the back row turned around.

Pastor Jack suddenly found himself staring into the most hideous face he had ever seen. Because of leprosy, this woman had no nose and no lips. And when she raised her hand to make a request, there was no hand there. Just a bony nub.

The woman said, "Could we sing 'Count Your Many Blessings'?"

Pastor Jack stood there at the podium, unable to speak, the tears welling up and choking off his voice. Finally, he had to step outside and weep. Another member of the group led the song. One of the men walked outside and put his arm around his pastor. "You'll never sing that song again, will you, Jack?" Jack said, "Oh yeah. But not in the same way."

Chapter Two

It Takes A Long Time to Become Young

"Old age is like everything else--to make a success of it, you've got to start young." *--Theodore Roosevelt*

In his 80s and 90s Konrad Adenauer was chancellor of West Germany. One day, receiving a physical examination when he was almost ninety, his doctor said, "Excellency, I'm not a magician. I can't make you younger." Adenauer said, "I haven't asked you to make me younger. I just want to go on getting older!"

In 1966 in Cannes, France, a museum was hosting a Pablo Picasso retrospective. Hundreds of canvasses were on display, arranged in chronological order. As one entered the building, the first works were done when Picasso was an adolescent. These were conventional landscapes and still lifes. They were proper and conservative.

Further into the hall, the canvasses changed. The landscapes came alive and took on new colors. Still lifes became less still. The artist was finding his voice.

Turn the corner. Now, you are in the mature period of Picasso's life, the period of cubism, acrobatics, bold experiments. The artist was freer and more alive than ever.

As told by Garson Kanin, the artist was moving throughout the museum, greeting each guest, enjoying the exhibit more than anyone. He wore red velvet trousers, a green silk jacket, and matching accessories. He was bubbling, laughing. Beautiful young women adorned each arm.

A woman friend approached Picasso and greeted him. He kissed her hand. They embraced. She said, "Master! It is formidable! It is stupendous!"

"Yes, yes," said the great artist.

The woman says, "But I do not understand the arrangement."

"Oh?"

"Well, the first pictures--the ones you painted as a youth--are so mature, so serious and solemn. And then the later ones, from your mature years, are extremely different and wild. It's almost as if the dates should be reversed. As if they are backward. How do you explain that?"

Picasso said, "Easily. It takes a long time to become young."

Garson Kanin liked that line so much he made it the title of his book on aging. I confess to loving it myself. So much so that, even though I read the book a generation ago, in preparation for our writing this little volume I went online and purchased a copy just so I could read it again.

Scripture promises something along this very line. It's the last few verses of Psalm 92...

"They will still bear fruit in old age. They will be full of sap and very green, to declare that the Lord is upright. He is my Rock, and there is no unrighteousness in Him."

God is promising and predicting that those who live for Him through the years, enjoying what Eugene

Peterson called "a long obedience in the same direction," will be fruitful in their old age, as well as youthful, beautiful, and truthful. I'm for that!

Chapter Three

I Was Wrong About Old Age

Like everyone else, I had dreaded old age. When I turned 20, it occurred to me the next big birthday would mean I was turning 30. Thirty?! That sounded like a hundred. And when I turned 30, the next big one would be forty! Forty!! Well, you know how that went....

Eventually, I turned fifty and the next big one would be sixty. And sixty felt like all the years in the world. After that, it gets heavier and darker: seventy, eighty, and into infinity!

Imagine my surprise. Seventy wasn't bad at all. In fact, it wasn't anything. Just a number.

I was so wrong. I had thought that being 70 or 80, etc., meant one was old! And out of it. And decrepit. Senile. Infirmed.

I never knew you could accumulate a lot of years and still be young and alive. Energetic and creative.

I never knew just how fleeting a century of years can be. I think back to when I was in college (1958-62). I worked weekends as a clerk-typist/dispatcher for the Pullman Company at the railroad terminal in Birmingham. In 1961, porters and conductors coming into our office would drop off the Sunday edition of the Atlanta newspaper. And that paper had begun reproducing the front page of their newspaper a hundred years earlier, during the Civil War. As a history major, I found this fascinating. Where I was wrong, however, was thinking of the Civil War as ancient history. A full century! But I was wrong. It was so very near.

Consider that when I was born--1940--hundreds of Civil War veterans still lived. And veterans of the Great War (aka, WWI) were still young men. And these days--I'm writing in 2018--we find ourselves celebrating the centennial of the end of that war.

My four grandparents were born in the 1880s and 1890s. My own grandchildren were born exactly a hundred years later. Now, consider that these children may well live into the 2080s. So, there is a real sense in which my life touches 200 hundred years. Back in

1976 we celebrated the bicentennial of America. Two hundred years felt like a millennium. But in truth, it's such a brief time.

I met someone who was one handshake away from Abraham Lincoln. A United Methodist pastor in North Carolina told me that in 1955 he was serving a church in the Midwest and had an elderly member from Gettysburg, Pennsylvania. In the fall of 1863 when President Lincoln came to their town to dedicate the cemetery, she was 10 years old. She and her mother had sat on the front row and thus had upfront seats to hear Lincoln's Gettysburg Address. Afterwards, they shook hands with President Lincoln.

So, when I shook his hand, I was two handshakes away from our greatest president.

In my lifetime, I have met Mitsuo Fuchida and General Paul Tibbetts, the two men who--in a very real way--began and ended the U.S. involvement in the Second World War. Fuchida was in charge of the Japanese fleet that bombed Pearl Harbor on December 7, 1941. And Tibbetts piloted the *Enola Gay* that dropped the atomic bomb on Hiroshima in August of 1945.

So many amazing things. Such a short lifetime.

This makes me wonder what else I was wrong about concerning aging and getting old...

--I was wrong in thinking old people are all "elderly." Many are youthful and spry and energetic and playful.

--I was wrong in thinking grownups are all a special creation, far different from the younger people around them. In time I came to realize there are no grownups. We are all children.

--There are some centenarians who have never been old a day in their lives. I've known several of them. One of my favorite friends, Nannie Kate Smith of Columbus, MS, was telling jokes at her 100th birthday party.

When I get old, I want to be young like that!

"Lord, teach us to number our days that we may apply our hearts unto wisdom" (Psalm 90:12).

Chapter Four

What Are You Waiting For? The Clock Is Ticking.

"All children, except one, grow up. They soon know that they will grow up, and the way Wendy knew was this. One day when she was two years old she was playing in a garden, and she plucked another flower and ran with it to her mother. I suppose she must have looked rather delightful, for Mrs. Darling put her hand to her heart and cried, 'Oh, why can't you remain like this forever!' This was all that passed between them on the subject, but henceforth Wendy knew that she must grow up. You always know that after you are two. Two is the beginning of the end."

Thus did J. M. Barrie begin the delightful story of Peter Pan.

Since it's safe to assume Wendy Darling was off in her calculations by a few decades, the question lingers: At what point do we actually start on the downside of life?

Some authorities say the decade between 65 and 75 is the youth of old age, from 75 to 85 is the maturity of old age, and from 85 on, well--you're old. I suppose that is right, although life has a way of moving those categories forward and upward. Those of us born before World War II can recall when you were old at 40!

Even so, we're realists. We know our earthly existence has a beginning and an ending. "Use by (date)" could well have been stamped on us when we arrived in this world.

We in the Western world live in a youth-oriented/age-denying culture that is most uncomfortable with the elderly and with the concept of growing old. When our favorite celebrities realized they were getting old, many of them took one of two unfortunate paths: they checked out early (suicide) or they underwent plastic surgery to camouflage the effects of time. We are disappointed when either happens. How much better, we feel, if our favorite stars had grown old gracefully and worn their crinkled skin and white hair as badges of lives well lived. What an example they would have set for their fans and admirers. This assumes, of course, that they found what makes life work well in the first place.

A famous preacher used to tell how when he was small, his mother taught him piano. Once in a recital, his mind froze up and he had to walk off the stage in total humiliation. Later, his mother gave him some advice.

"Darling," she said, "anytime you mess up in the middle of a number you're playing, always end with a flourish and no one will remember what you did in the middle."

That preacher would look out at his congregation and say, "Some of you may have messed up in the middle. But you don't have to end that way, friend. There's still time to get it right, to end with a flourish."

None of us have gotten it right all the way without messing up once. We are all sinners who have come short of the grace of God.

We all had to learn to humble ourselves and come to Him in repentance, to receive His grace and then get back out there and finish what we had started.

So, if that's you, if you are one who needs to do something in order to "finish with a flourish," we have a question for you:

What are you waiting for?

Now is the time.

Scripture says, "This is the day the Lord has made; I will rejoice and be glad in it." That's Psalm 118:24.

"Now is the accepted time; today is the day of salvation." 2 Corinthians 6:2.

"Today if you hear His voice, harden not your heart." Repeated three times in the Epistle to the Hebrews. It's in 3:7; 3:15; and 4:7.

So then, back to our question...

What are you waiting for?

If you know God's will for you, what's keeping you from stepping up to the plate and taking a swing at it? To go for it.

"Let's do this."

I've heard that Ty Cobb, the famous baseball player from Georgia, came to know the Lord Jesus a few weeks before he died of cancer in Atlanta's Grady Hospital. The man had put in 22 years with the Detroit Tigers and set a ton of records, some of which are still on the books. But if Cobb was a great player, he was also one of the rudest. He had an attitude; no one liked him much. But after he came to know Christ, he sent a message to the men he'd played ball with. "Fellows, I got in the bottom of the ninth. I sure wish I'd come in the top of the first."

I told that story once down in Valdosta, Georgia, and a senior lady came up afterwards. "I was Ty Cobb's nurse in Grady Hospital before he died. He was the sweetest man!"

You never know.

What are you waiting for?

I actually know the answer to the question.

Often people will tell us preachers, "I'm going to start living for the Lord, Pastor. One of these days."

Sound familiar?

"One of these days" may be the biggest scam in the universe. If you're on the internet, you know about scams. But this one is the biggest because it comes right out of hell. Satan knows you're too smart for him to say, "Tell that preacher I'm going to die and go to hell." You'd say, "Oh no. I'm not going to do that!" So, he takes a different route to the same end. "Tell that preacher you're going to do it, but just not today." And you fall for it.

You'll get up tomorrow and look at yourself in the mirror and say, "I'm going to get my life right with God, but not today." And the next morning you'll say, "Just not today." And eventually, you run out of days.

You've heard that the road to hell is paved with good intentions. Hell itself is populated with people who had good intentions. They had planned to get saved and live for God. They just never got around to it.

A family asked me to go see their elderly grandfather. "Grandpa has been putting off preachers down through the years. And now he's old and sickly and the doctors say he's not long for this world." I drove to the hospital and found his room.

The old gentleman was small and weak and plugged into all kinds of machines. I introduced myself and told him that some of his family asked me to come by and talk with him about Jesus. "Could I do that?" He nodded his head. He was very polite.

I told him what God had done for him in Christ. After a bit I said, "Sir, would you like me to pray with you and ask Jesus Christ to come into your life and forgive your sins and make you a child of God? He would write your name down in the book of life and receive you as one of His own. Could we do that?"

The old man could barely whisper. "I'm going to do that, preacher. One of these days."

I felt like saying, "Sir, you've used up all your days. You don't have any left." But I knew what had happened. He got so used to saying that over the years that now when he's standing at the edge of the precipice, about to go over, he can't turn it off.

That's why Scripture says, "Today if you hear His voice, harden not your heart."

Granted, it doesn't feel like you're hardening your heart. All you're doing is telling the Lord "later, not today." But it's rebellion, friend.

Remember when you were a little kid? Go back to when you were ten years old. Suppose your mama came into your bedroom and said, "This room looks like a tornado went through. Get up right now and clean it up!" And suppose you said, "I will clean it up...one of these days." Is that rebellion? You bet it is. And she wouldn't put up with it.

You might try telling your mom what people say to the Lord: "I'll do it when I get the feeling."

She'll give you the feeling.

What is keeping you from opening your heart to the Lord Jesus Christ at this moment and putting faith and trust in Him?

It's not rocket science, friend. It's so simple a child can do it. Pause and talk to the Lord. Tell Him you are repenting of your sin to the best of your ability and you want to start anew with Jesus as the Lord and Master of your life. Starting this minute.

Chapter Five

These advanced years provide us more time and opportunities.

We're fully aware that everyone's situation is different. Plenty of seniors are still working to put groceries on the table and pay the rent. Some are having to raise their grandchildren and see no foreseeable time when retirement is an option. God bless them! And, from time to time we meet people in their 80s and beyond who still hold down full-time jobs just because they're able and love what they do. So, we're speaking generally here when we say that these so-called golden years provide time and opportunities for us to do some things.

A. We have time to pray. Some years ago, a dear friend had to go into an assisted living center, and later into the nursing home. She told me, Bertha, one day that she thanked the Lord for all the time she had to pray. She had always wished she had more time to pray, and now she does.

B. We have time to share our faith with others. Wherever we are, at any time or place, there is always someone with whom we can share our faith in Jesus Christ. Bertha builds relationships with neighbors by taking them banana bread she has baked. Joe sketches people at every opportunity and uses this as an opportunity to witness.

C. Many of us will have the opportunity to do missionary service. Becky Crumpton, a classmate of Joe's brother Ron, has devoted her years after retiring as a high school teacher to mission trips, in the U.S. and elsewhere. Once when Joe was speaking to the Alabama Baptist Convention, just before he rose to speak, they recognized Becky as the "Alabama Volunteer of the Year." And she was 75! Truly amazing.

From a young child, I, Bertha, had always desired to become a missionary, maybe to Africa or Brazil. During college, I attended a weekly "Mission Prayer Band" where several hundred other students met. Missionaries spoke, and we sang mission hymns. I became eager to go anywhere, and my heart would be filled to bursting. However, as soon as I left the building, the feeling would go away. Others always seemed passionate as I saw them around campus. I wondered why my passion for missions did not remain.

Then, after graduating, the Lord gave me a wonderful husband who was called to be a pastor. In our first year of marriage when we were almost 22, our apartment was directly across the street from a very large church, one with a mission-oriented emphasis that permeated everything the church did. Once a year, they had a week-long mission conference, which occurred soon after we had moved there. We attended every night. One night we told each other that we both were feeling a call to missions, to Africa or Brazil! We knelt, wept and prayed together, telling the Lord that we would go wherever He chose to send us. Almost the moment we stood up, we both sensed the "burden" was lifted. Neither of us understood at the time, but over the years we learned that the Lord wanted us to be willing and that He would choose for us the best time and place for us to minister. In all of our pastorates, we were able to take our members on mission trips in the States and overseas. Then, when we were in our 50's, we began sensing a need to go overseas. However, this was delayed as some of the doors to countries we were looking at were closed. Finally, when we were 60, the Lord opened the door with the SBC's International Mission Board for us to go under the Master's Program (for those over 50). We chose a position in Malawi, Africa, which seemed to suit us best, and we were approved to fill a one-year term until a career missionary arrived. What a "harvest" we saw; how blessed we were. Afterwards, we were home for six months when a position became available in Brasilia, Brazil, where we served for four years.

D. *At this age, we're able to pass along treasured personal items to friends and family.* A great time to do this is when downsizing and moving into an assisted living residence or even a nursing home. However, it is more fun to give these items away earlier when we are still active and in good health and can enjoy placing them in just the right spot.

When our mother died, my sister and I invited our children to go through her belongings and choose something that reminded them of Grandmother. The only piece our son asked for was a little telephone stand that was quite worn. It was where Grandmother had sat when she talked with him on the phone.

After our children were grown and on their own, each time we moved, we gave them some of our things. When we left to serve in Malawi, we had to store our furnishings in a warehouse. Since there was not room for everything, again we let them pick out some items. Storing our two cars was very expensive for the year. Later, before going to serve in Brazil, my brother-in-law said, "Why not give these to your children now while they need and can use them." We did that and never regretted it.

If we are fortunate to have money we would like to give our children, we certainly should consider it. However, money is not the most important blessing we pass on to our families. A legacy of faith, holiday traditions, and great memories are treasures that do not fade with time.

E. *In these senior years, we have the opportunity to influence our children, grandchildren, friends.* It's like "passing the baton" in a relay race. We model for them even when we cannot physically do anything for them. My sister and I often talk about something we saw our mother do years ago when we were growing up. She loved to pray, and people would come to her for prayer. Even when she was in a nursing home with severe dementia, she had such a gentle, caring spirit. Other patients and even the nurses and staff would come to her for prayer. One day when Laura and I were in the room, a staff member walked in and asked Mother to pray for her. She knelt down beside Mother's wheelchair and held Mother's hand as they prayed together. Mother's prayers were always as if she were perfectly healthy without the slightest evidence of dementia, just sincere and full of concern for the specific need, talking to our Heavenly Father. We always were mystified but blessed at the same time.

F. We can volunteer. They're needing workers at the local homeless shelter. We can ask the pastor what needs tending to around the church. Many churches will have seniors answering the phones, one day a week per senior. It's not stressful, it can be a lot of fun, and it takes a load off the office staff.

And we can read the books we've been saving for when we "have the time." Go back and read some of the classics you wish you'd read when you were young. Start with Jane Austen's *Pride and Prejudice*, my all-time favorite.

We can travel and see some of the great parks in the land. As a baseball fan, I recommend checking out the baseball parks around the country.

We can do a thousand things. This can be the best years of our lives if we will quit making excuses and be obedient to the Father.

What we must not do is keep putting off doing these things for some perfect time. There will be no ideal moment to do something you've wanted to do for years. Just decide and go for it!

Chapter Six

Some great Scriptures about this time of our lives...

--"White hair is a crown of glory and is seen most among the godly" (Proverbs 16:31).

--"The glory of young men is their strength; of old men (and women), their experience" (Proverbs 20:29).

--"Teach a child to choose the right path, and when he is older he will remain upon it" (Proverbs 22:6).

--"You must teach others those things you and many others have heard me speak about. Teach these great truths to trustworthy men who will, in turn, pass them on to others" (II Timothy 2:2).

--"You have been chosen by God Himself--you are priests of the King, you are holy and pure, you are God's very own--all this so that you may show to others how God called you out of the darkness into His wonderful light" (I Peter 2:9).

--"O God, You have taught me from my youth; and to this day I declare Your wondrous works. Now also when I am old and gray headed, O God, do not forsake me, until I declare Your strength to this generation, Your power to everyone who is to come" (Psalm 71:17-18).

--"I will reveal these truths to you so that you can describe these glorious deeds of Jehovah to your children and tell them about the mighty miracles He did" (Psalm 78:4).

--"Let each generation tell its children what glorious things He does" (Psalm 145:4).

--"Be very careful never to forget what you have seen God doing for you. May His miracles have a deep and permanent effect upon your lives! Tell your children and your grandchildren about the glorious miracles He did" (Deuteronomy 4:9).

--"So keep these commandments carefully in mind. . . teach them to your children. Talk about them when you are sitting at home, when you are out walking, at bedtime, and before breakfast!" (Deuteronomy 11:18, 19).

--"He commanded our fathers to teach these truths to our children so that they in turn could teach their children too" (Psalm 78:6).

--"I have been young, and now am old; yet I have not seen the righteous forsaken, nor his descendants begging bread. He is ever merciful and lends; And his descendants are blessed" (Psalm 37:25-26).

--"Now Joshua was old, advanced in years. And the Lord said to him, 'You are old, advanced in years, and there remains much land yet to be possessed'" (Joshua 13:1).

--(Caleb is speaking) "And now behold, the Lord has kept me alive, as He said, these forty-five years, ever since the Lord spoke this word to Moses....and now, here I am this day, eighty-five years old. As yet I am as strong this day as on the day that Moses sent me.... Now therefore, give me this mountain...." (Joshua 14:10-12).

--"The righteous shall flourish like a palm tree; He shall grow like a cedar in Lebanon. Those who are planted in the house of the Lord shall flourish in the courts of our God. They shall still bear fruit in old age; They shall be fresh and flourishing (*literally: 'full of sap and very green'*); To declare that the Lord is upright, He is my Rock, and there is no unrighteousness in Him" (Psalm 92:12-15).

Chapter Seven

20 Things I Do Which May or May Not Be Keeping Me Young

(An article from Joe's blog earlier this year)

If you plan to stay around for the long term, you'll want to give attention to your health.

Psalm 92:14 promises that godly old people will still be young and fruitful in their old age, so I'm just claiming the promise! Okay, maybe that passage is just *predicting* it rather than *promising* it. Either way, I'm dedicated to making it a reality as far as I can.

So, taking inventory, here are some things I do. And don't miss the (ahem) truth in advertising statement at the end! Smiley-face goes here.

1. I laugh a lot. I love Genesis 21:6 where Sarah says, "God has made laughter for me." My friend Jerry Clower used to say, "There's only one place in the

universe where there will be no laughter. And I've made arrangements to miss it!"

2. I take a full regimen of vitamins every day. When a friend asked for a list of those pills, I declined. I'm no doctor and don't want to be prescribing anything for anyone. But 25 years ago, while having a rare checkup, my doctor ordered me to lose some weight, get back to walking, and to take a baby aspirin each day along with a multi-vitamin. Then she said, "Mr. McKeever, I think we've just prevented a heart attack in you." Evidently, she was right. I'm grateful.

3. I have an annual checkup, complete with bloodwork. One doctor told me the typical annual checkup that companies provide for their employees is "a handshake." For my money, it's the lab's running tests on the blood they draw from me that tells the story. They can tell a hundred things about one's health from a small blood sample.

4. I see my dentist twice a year. Back in 2004, it was the hygienist who found the oral cancer. So, it's not stretching things to say I owe my life to regular dental checkups!

5. I love to walk. Back when I was in my 30s, I joined the jogging craze. That came to an abrupt halt the day I got a stone bruise in my shin. When I was able to return to my schedule, I discovered that walking is far superior to jogging. While walking, I can think and talk to the Lord and go over a sermon I'm about to preach.

6. I read, read, read. I take the daily newspaper and a few journals. Other than that, I read novels (my favorite is a good western novel, or a Michael Connelly or Lee Child crime story) and histories, as well as the occasional book on spiritual things. Both my sons are readers, as is Bertha's daughter. So, we often pass books around in the family.

7. I pray all the time. I get a kick out of those surveys which say the average person prays only 45 seconds a day or whatever. At the end of my day, if someone asked how long I prayed, I might answer, "How long did I talk to my wife? We talked all day long." And so with prayer. "Pray without ceasing," Scripture says.

8. I work puzzles. Jigsaw puzzles and word puzzles, and sometimes crossword puzzles. My favorite jigsaw

puzzles are cartoons done by a wonderful Dutch artist Jan van Haasteren. Google him. He's amazing.

9. I blog. We started our website in the early 2000s. So now our blog has over 3,000 articles, almost all devoted to pastors and other church leaders. It is never far from my mind and gives me a great outlet for a constant stream of thoughts, concerns, insights, and inspirations.

10. I draw cartoons for publications. To see a few thousand of my drawings, go to the Baptist Press website www.bpnews.net and click on "comics."

11. I'm a sketch artist and I draw lots of people. Sometimes, it's by invitation for a convention or a party or church supper, but often it's spontaneous. In the breakfast room at hotels, I'll sketch employees and guests.

12. I'm a preacher. I preach many times a year and am always working on improving my sermons.

13. I'm married to a youthful, energetic, resourceful wife. Every day is a surprise.

14. I'm surrounded by friends. When traveling through distant cities where I have friends, we'll call them in advance to meet us for coffee or lunch. Bertha says she's constantly amazed at how many friends I have. "And they're all so classy," she says. I remind her she has yet to meet all my kinfolk.

15. Between the two of us, we have 14 grandchildren. And of course, five children. Interestingly, three of the five are adopted (her two and my daughter). But these days it's the grands who keep us laughing and traveling to graduations and weddings.

16. I love nature. In our back yard is a pond where a great blue heron comes daily. We have bird feeders by our back deck. Bertha does flowers and grows tomatoes and blueberries by the house.

17. We have a dog. Enough said.

18. I try to eat right. Just as I'm not in the business of prescribing vitamins or anything else, I'm no dietician, so don't look for a long list of kitchen rules here. But my main recommendation is to keep fruits on hand. This morning, in our cheerios we had strawberries and blueberries. In a bowl on the table was a sliced-

up peach (this is July and the peaches are wonderful!). We have bananas and a few cannisters containing nuts (peanuts, almonds, cashews).

19. Bertha and I have a few television programs we watch together and enjoy immensely. She got me started on "Blue Bloods" as well as "Father Brown" and "Madame Secretary." Those are must-sees on our schedule.

20. When praying, I ask the Father for good health. Recently, when a granddaughter asked how she could pray for me, I said, "Pray the Lord will keep me in good health so I can go on preaching and living and loving into my 90s!" She said, "I already pray that." Good. Thank you, honey.

This is not to say I do everything right....

I'm not a poster child for discipline-in-healthcare. I suspect you may want to do as I say, not as I do, as the old joke goes.

I don't always eat right, I love ice cream like few people have ever loved it! I love a Little Debbie cake and even though Bertha disputes this, I'm basically a very lazy person. So, I may not be the best role model!

I read the same health advisories you do, I suppose. Some will say that a person around 5'10" or 5'11" should weigh something like 150 pounds. I read that and think, "What? I weighed that when we married, and Margaret said I was skin and bones and she was going to fatten me up!" My dad fought the battle of a bulging waistline most of his adult life and lived to be nearly 96 years old. Maybe if he'd weighed less, he could have lived to be 110. The experts have a lot of learning to do on this subject, I'm thinking.

So, bottom line--for me at least--is do the best you can, don't beat yourself up too severely over that extra dessert once in a while, and stay active. You and your spouse can help each other on this. And if you are widowed or single, invite a friend to join a conspiracy of health with you.

A post script to this chapter--

Bertha, younger than me by five months, is a poster child for staying youthful all the way home. This wonderful wife of mine is a great cook, loves to have people over to the house for a meal or a weekend, she works in the yard with flowers, grows tomatoes and blueberries, she is a seamstress, and she cuts my hair! She crochets afghans for family members and women at a local ministry, and bakes banana bread for shut-ins. She is truly amazing. (I tell her the $23 I spent for that marriage license was the bargain of the year!) Meanwhile, she's still teaching English at the local community college. She has a prayer list a mile long and may be the finest Christian I've ever known.

Dr. S. B. Platt of Columbus, Mississippi, graduated from medical school in 1940, the year we were born. He practiced medicine until he was 83. He told me once that from time to time a patient will complain that he "has no energy for sex." Dr. Platt would ask, "What kind of exercise are you getting?" The patient would say, "Doc, you don't understand. I don't have energy!" To that, the wise old medic would say, "My friend, to have energy you must use energy. Get busy exercising and you will have more energy for everything!"

Some of the best advice concerning our physical well-being is the old adage "Use it or lose it." At any age, if we are not using particular muscles it's as though the body says, "If you're not going to be needing it, we'll shut it down." Suddenly, when you find yourself needing that muscle, it's no longer there.

The only way to keep muscle tone and plenty of energy is to stay active. Use those muscles. Walk, exercise, stretch. The dividends will be enormous.

"PASTOR DAVIDSON, YOU ARE DELIBERATELY ENDANGERING YOUR HEALTH BY GETTING OLDER."
SILLY ME. WHAT WAS I THINKING?
LAB REPORT

Chapter Eight

Grandparenting Is Just About the Best Thing Ever. Here Are A Few Thoughts on The Subject.

If you are about to become a grandparent for the first time, you are about to be more in love than you have ever been in your life.

While it's still "in the oven," you don't even know that child. But a few months from now, you won't be able to live without it! Life is wonderful that way.

Having your first grandchild is just that strong an attachment, that huge a reality, that big a game-changer.

We--Bertha and Joe--have 14 grandchildren between us. In birth order: Leah, Jessica, Allison, Grant, Megan, Abigail, Erin, Darilyn, Shannon, JoAnne, Ethan, Jack, Juliet, and Zoe. These young people get prayed for every day. They are dearer to us than they could ever know.

We share grandparenting roles (and duties and privileges) with others, of course. And we're happy to do so. Grandmother Betty Gatwood, called "MawMaw" by three of the above, takes them to New York City to shop and sightsee and enjoy Broadway plays. Margaret and I could never have done that, so we're thrilled that Betty could and does. (I've suggested to her more than once that she and Ray adopt me!)

When Grant was born, his dad Neil put a baby swing in the front yard and said, "That is Grandpa's place." I happily took him up on it. A couple of years later when Abby and Erin came along, the swing got more and more use. Eventually, we replaced it with a big-kid swing and the spot under the tree was worn down to the ground. Sometimes in the middle of a tough day of pastoring, I would run by the house just for a few minutes. Those three would bolt out the back door, calling "Me first! Me first!" I'd spend five minutes with one--laughing, telling stories, making up songs, anything. Then, the next child would take the swing and we'd do the same thing over again. It was better than any medicine ever invented.

Abby was six years old. We were at the swing, laughing and cutting up and having a big time. She said, "We're being silly, aren't we, Grandpa?" I said, "Yes, we are. Why do we like to be so silly?" She said, "It's a family tradition."

When Abby and Erin were eight, their mother Julie was teaching them about child-birth. One day when we were at the swing, Abby abruptly said, "Grandpa, I'm not going to have any children. It hurts too bad." Well, I thought, who can argue with that? The price mothers pay to bring their little ones into the world is an amazing thing. But, if they weren't willing to make such a sacrifice, none of us would be here. I thought of saying all these things but didn't. What I said was, "Yes, it does hurt. But the pain goes away, and you're left with this beautiful child and you decide that it was worth it."

She was quiet a moment, then said, "You're a man. What do you know?"

I fell on the grass laughing so hard. "You're exactly right," I said. "All I know is what the women have told me, and they may have been lying."

Granddaughter Erin gave me a story I used after Hurricane Katrina ravaged the Gulf Coast and put so many of our neighborhoods and churches out of business. One day Neil had told the children to be praying for beautiful weather the next day. "If it's a pretty day, we'll go to the park."

Next day they were in his pickup heading over to LaFreniere Park. Neil said, "I want to know who asked God to give us this beautiful day. Grant, did you?" "No, I forgot," he said.

"Abby, did you?" "No, I forgot too."

Erin called out from the back seat, "Oh good. Then it was my miracle!"

After Katrina, as point-man for the SBC churches of metro New Orleans, my office was ground zero for rebuilding churches and hundreds of homes. As a result, I was invited all over to speak of what God was doing in our city. At the conclusion of my report, I would tell them Erin's story, then say, "One of these days, the Lord will have done in New Orleans whatever He has planned. And if you came to help us, if you sent money, if you prayed for us, or helped in any other way, New Orleans will be your miracle."

Ask any pastor. Grandchildren stories are the best!

Dot Green gave me one about her sister's granddaughter which I have used ever since. The grandmother was talking to her 5-year-old about the child's teenage sister who had taken up cigarette-smoking. She said, "Honey, I hope you won't ever take up that filthy habit." The child said, "Grandma, that's one thing you don't ever have to worry about. I don't ever plan to smoke.... unless I'm drunk."

Okay, I didn't exactly say it's a sermon illustration but it's a great story. I suppose it could work in a sermon, under the right circumstances.

Here are a few pointers on the business of grandparenting.

1. You can pray. Pray for them every day, even though you will not have a clue how the Lord answered you. Just believe that He has, that He is, and that He will. And therefore, you will pray about the future of those children. Pray for them as young adults, all the choices they'll be making. Pray for them as grownups, their

spouses, their jobs, their own children, and such. Above all, pray they will know the Lord Jesus Christ and live for Him every day of their lives.

When you get to Heaven, you will find out how vital those prayers were!

2. You are a backup resource for the parents. Sometimes that means babysitting, sometimes it means money, and it always means encouragement and love.

3. You can talk to the children, telling them stories of your childhood, how you learned certain lessons in unforgettable ways. Once when some of my grandchildren rode with me from New Orleans to Nauvoo, Alabama to see my parents, later they reported to their mom and dad, "Grandpa talked the whole way." I smiled at that, because while it wasn't literally true, I did have a lot of things I wanted to plant in those young fertile minds and talking is a great way to do it.

4. You can teach them crafts you have learned. Woodworking, hunting and fishing, golf, boating, the list is endless. I confess to having tried to teach Grant

to draw cartoons from the time he was an infant. As far as we can tell, it didn't "take." But it was fun nevertheless!

5. You can take the children on trips. When our three New Orleans grands were in elementary school, Margaret and I took them on a train ride to Birmingham. There we rented a car and drove to the country and visited with my parents for 36 hours. Then, we retraced our steps. They still remember it.

6. Be a counselor and sounding board for the children. Particularly as they become teens, this can be a vital role.

7. You can write a Grandparents' Book. Here are Bertha's thoughts on that....

I suppose this is one of my most cherished items. About 20 years ago one of our church members in Melbourne, Florida, brought me a book she had ordered for us. Our first grandchild was about two, so she thought I needed to begin making a record for this child and all future grandchildren. It is a huge, beautiful book of 365 large pages. The book asks questions of one's entire life--your childhood, your fondest memories, your best friends, everything. Any of us would love to have such a book written by a cherished grandparent or even great-grandparent.

When I started the book, I wrote in the front, "I am now 57 years old, of sound mind and body. I am beginning with the last page in the book and will work toward the first page, knowing that if I start at the front I will never finish; I will plan to write one page per day so as to complete it in 365 days!" I kept to it and finished it on time--whew!!!

8. Keep a journal. Joe kept a daily journal for the decade of the 1990s (his 50's). Eventually, it filled over 50 hard-bound books. It has a complete record of his and Margaret's lives during those years and covers every incident that occurred in the family, including the births of most of the grandchildren. As the little ones grew up, when they did something funny or memorable, he wrote it in the book. It's a treasured keepsake.

I read once that we do not keep journals for our children. Presumably, they lived through those same periods with us and will not be curious about what we write. But journals are for grandchildren and beyond. I agree.

The bad news about grandchildren...

--They grow up. First thing you know, they're graduating from high school and going off to college or joining the military and moving far from you. This is one of the toughest adjustments you will ever have to make at this time in your life.

--As they grow up, you become less and less the center of their lives. When they were preschoolers, it was their parents and siblings and you. Gradually, teachers and classmates entered the picture. And by the time they are teens, we grandparents are less and less a part of their daily lives. It feels cruel, but you did the same thing with your grandparents. It's called life.

--So, you make the adjustment and keep praying for them. Phone them once in a while. Find out what social media they use and join it, if for no other reason just to stay in touch with them that way.

Chapter Nine

What God Wants You (And Me) To Know About the Rest of Our Lives...

Half the people I know claim as their favorite scripture Jeremiah 29:11. "For I know the plans I have for you, declares the Lord, plans for your welfare and not for calamity, to give you a future and a hope." It's a great verse.

That promise was given to Israel in exile in Babylon. The entire 29th chapter has the whole story, but it's worth a mention here. False prophets had arisen in Babylon doing what false prophets do best: Tell people what they want to hear. And what these homesick, displaced Jews wanted to hear was that they were returning to Judah very soon. So, the con men stepped up to tell them just that. Meanwhile, down in Jerusalem, God dictated this letter to Jeremiah and had him send it by a couple of messengers.

God said to His people in exile: "You are going to be in Babylon for seventy years. So, unpack your bags, build houses, plant gardens, have weddings, and have babies. And work for the welfare of the city where I have sent you into exile. After all, as it prospers, you will prosper." (29:5-7).

The people were shocked. Seventy years?!! Oh no! That's a lifetime. So, the Lord gave them the good news: He was still with them, watching over them, and making plans for them. (verse 11 fits here.)

All of this applies to us. It fits us perfectly. We are here for a period of time and must not camp out on a mountaintop waiting for His return. We are to be about the Father's business. In that vein--whether we are 17 years old or 75 years young--here are five things the living God wants you and me to know about the rest of our lives....

--One: He has big plans for us. Earthly plans (such as making us the light of the world, the salt of the earth, showing forth His praises through us, spreading the gospel) and heavenly plans ("I go to prepare a place for you," Jesus said).

--Two: He's not going to tell us what those plans are. Why not? Because the really difficult stuff, we couldn't handle. Suppose I had known a year in advance that my wife would die in January of 2015. I would have cried for a solid year and her last days would have been awful. As it was, it was a very good year. The last day of her life, we spent an hour at the breakfast table sharing, talking, and praying. And, then, the really great stuff, if we knew that in advance, we'd probably mess it up.

--Three: He's getting us ready for the future right now. What we are going through is to prepare us for His work through us in this life and to further prepare us for Heaven.

--Four: Our task is to be faithful today where He has placed us, to bloom where we were planted. We pastors run into people all the time who say they could serve the Lord if their circumstances were different. If they had a better job, lived in a different city, were married to someone else (or not married!), or had a bigger income. I've even had people say to me, "I know I'm not sharing my faith in Christ here at home, but if I were a missionary in some foreign country, I would." My answer is a succinct, "No, you wouldn't."

--Five: But we have to choose every day of our lives to accept His blessings. He does not force Heaven's blessings on anyone. He said to Jerusalem, "How often I would have gathered you together like a mother hen gathers its baby chicks and loves on them...but you were unwilling" (Matthew 23:37). I love this insight from Revelation 3:20. "Behold, I stand at your door and knock; if anyone hear my voice and open the door, I will come in...." We have here the most amazing picture: The Lord Jesus brings Heaven's blessings right up to our door but no further. He knocks and asks for permission to bless us.

"As for me and my house, said Joshua, we will serve the Lord" (Joshua 24: 15). We choose to serve Him!

Whether seniors or juniors, each of us should get up every morning of our lives and make ourselves available for the Lord's blessings for that day. I heard Rick Warren say every morning he asks, "Lord, are you going to be doing anything important today? I sure would like to be in on it!"

Chapter Ten

Everyone Wonders: "Should A Widowed Senior Remarry or Not?" Obviously, We Have Some Thoughts on The Subject.

(Note: So many seniors are widowed during these golden years, we wrote an entire book on the subject. "Grief Recovery 101" is the story of what we both went through in losing our spouses of 52 years, how we recovered, what we learned, etc.)

A book for seniors ought to address the subject of remarriage, don't you think? When we were considering marriage, I asked friends far and wide if they knew of a book advising widowed seniors on marrying again. No one did. So, we will devote a little extra space in this book for the subject. We hope it will help someone.

I can't approach this subject without remembering an older gentleman from an earlier pastorate who became widowed and then made the mistake of his life. A few months after his wife died, he was hospitalized for something, fell in love with his nurse, and within a few weeks had married her. She may have been half his age. I will confess that we all wondered what she saw in him. In time, we found out. She cleaned out his bank account and disappeared, never to be seen again.

So, when I counsel with older folks on the subject of remarrying, I urge them to slow down and take their own good time about it. There is no need to rush into it. Better a few months well-married than many years of misery!

There are lots of reasons for seniors to remarry......

I asked Bertha to help me come up with all the reasons why seniors should consider getting married.

We are aware of the statistics. Women will live longer than men and so there will be more widows than available widowers. Even so, for those who are interested, here are our "reasons to consider getting married as seniors."

1. You have more living to do.

2. You're not ready for the grave yet.

3. You have much to share, to do, to give.

4. You need some laughter in your life.

5. You need a close friend in the best sense of the word.

6. Married people help one another to stay safe and healthy. That's why married people tend to live longer.

7. You'll have someone to talk to and to listen.

8. It's great to be in love again. See below.

9. You can always use another point of view.

10. You need companionship.

11. Living as a couple is cheaper. Maybe.

12. Bertha added, "You need someone to tell you that you're special. Very, very special." (I'm happy to fill that role for her.)

13. Being married may take a burden off your adult children. They'd been worried about you living alone, and suddenly you're not any longer.

When I'd been widowed maybe a year, my older brother Ron, a pastor in the Birmingham area, said, "When seniors marry, it's for companionship." I said, "Not me. If I marry again, it will be for love."

When Bertha and I met, Margaret had been in Heaven for 13 months. Bertha's husband of 52 years, Gary Fagan, had been with the Lord nearly 2 years.

We knew that week that God had put us together.

Yes, we were in love.

Once, after we married, we traveled forty miles to the cemetery where Gary is buried. We bought flowers and took them to his grave. At one point, as Bertha knelt there, I walked away to give her space. Later she said, "It should tell you how much I love you because I loved him so much."

Sometimes she and I give each other notes on "50 reasons I love you." It's fun thinking of the reasons.

We do a lot of things together, but we still have our own separate lives. Bertha is still teaching English for a local community college (most always online). Sometimes she sits at the laptop for hours on end reading and grading papers. But that's fine, because on the other side of the table I'm writing articles for various publications and drawing cartoons for Baptist Press and the occasional special request. When I preach somewhere on weekends, she almost always accompanies me. Having been the wife of a pastor for 52 years, Bertha loves to greet people at church and to pray for her preacher-husband as he shares the Lord's message.

Of course, not every senior should get married. There are lots of reasons for that, too!

You are enjoying your singleness. You would have to give up a lot of freedom. And your requirements in a spouse are so specific (demanding?) that you can't find anyone who measures up.

The best reason for not remarrying is that you don't want to. The worst reason for not marrying is that your family is against it for all the wrong reasons.

Here is a short list of reasons why seniors should not remarry....

1. You don't want to. (Okay, I said that already. But it's number one.)

2. You like your independence. Which is sort of number 1, I suppose.

3. The other person does not share your faith.

4. You cannot agree on basics, such as where you will live, where you will go to church, how you will handle finances, how to protect the assets of each person, etc.

5. One has serious health problems which would be too big a burden for the other.

6. One of you is pressuring the other to marry. Be strong and resist the pressure.

7. One of you has little financial resources and hopes the other will take care of you with his/her money. This is trouble in the making.

8. One of you is unwilling to get premarital counsel.

9. One of you is unwilling to work out a prenuptial agreement to protect the assets.

10. Reasonable and loving family members advise against it. (Note that above we said the worst reason not to remarry is that family members are against your remarriage *for all the wrong reasons*. But they may have

good reasons. So, if you would normally respect the counsel of these loved ones, it's probably a good idea to do so now.)

11. Your pastor advises against it.

Why remarriage is a great idea--even necessary! --for some people

"Two are better than one because they have a good return for their labor," says Ecclesiastes 4:9ff. If one falls, the other can lift them up. If they lie down together, they can warm up each other. And if someone can overpower one, two can withstand him. It's a great reminder.

My longtime friends Dick and Kathy Rollins are a few years younger than us, but they have retired and moved off to another state to be closer to the grands. Not long ago when I was preaching in the area and they had me over for dinner, Kathy said, "Joe, I've told our sons that Dick needs a wife. So, if I should go first, they should know it's all right with me for him to marry again." She paused and added, "But I've told him not to do it while I'm lying in the casket in the other room!" We all laughed.

Some people desperately need the completeness and (a lot of other things; I'm not sure what all!) which only marriage can provide.

I ran across a great illustration of why marriage is a good idea from a book on the Civil War prison in Andersonville, Georgia. One of the worst penal institutions in history, Andersonville is where hundreds of Union soldiers died from disease and starvation. I've visited the grounds which is preserved by the National Parks Department. (McKinley Kantor's book *Andersonville* is the definitive work on the subject, even though it's a work of fiction.)

At various times prisoners would attempt to tunnel out of Andersonville. On a particular occasion the tunnel was long, and the diggers felt they might now be beyond the walls. Then one day an inmate walking across the prison yard fell into a hole. On investigating, they discovered that hole was the farthest point of their tunnel. Instead of burrowing a straight line across the yard and under the walls to the outside, the tunnel was shaped like an arc. Both the beginning and the end were inside the prison compound. What had happened?

All the diggers were right-handed. As they worked in the darkness, scraping with metal cans or whatever tools they had, they were curving the tunnel. In time, it would have been a giant circle!

The diggers needed a corrective, a counterbalance. Something to keep them focused on a straight path.

Most of us who have been married for decades have learned that marriage provides that counterbalance for us.

Two 2" x 4"s are stronger than one 4" x 4", we're told. The differing grains of the two pieces of wood reinforce each other.

Personally, I'm a better man married than single.

How to decide: should we marry or not?

You've met someone, and you care for him/her deeply. Should you get married? Here are some pointers for you to consider...

1. Slow down. Take your own time. Don't rush into marriage as some have done. We've all heard them say, "We don't have the luxury of a long engagement!" But better to take this slowly and deliberately than to

wake up and realize you have done something you regret.

2. Meet each other's friends. Look at him/her through the eyes of the friends. You'll learn a lot. Bertha said early on that all my friends seemed so classy. I would say, teasingly, "You haven't met my relatives!" (But I agree with her assessment. Friends like Earl and Maxine Stegall, Roy and Penny Lively, Anthony and Linda Kay, Jim and Darlene Graham, Joel and Wilma Davis--the list goes on and on. They are high quality people!)

3. At some point, take the "Prepare/Enrich" questionnaire. We did this through a counseling ministry here in the Jackson, MS area. They sent an email attachment containing the questionnaire. We took it (separately) and a week later sat in the office of the counselor who had collated the results. He handed us the charts showing how closely our answers agreed. We were almost identical on everything except the finances, but that was only because we'd not discussed money during our brief relationship. At the end, the counselor said, "You two are so perfectly matched. You don't need me." We

had felt that was the case, but we wanted an outside opinion.

4. Work on projects together. One day Bertha announced that she was ordering three bookcases for me as a wedding present. When they arrived, we were both surprised to see they were in long flat boxes. They had to be assembled! And the instructions were quite the challenge.

But we set in to tackle the project. I think the first one took four hours. We laughed and had fun. "Look! We have this part backwards!" and would have to take something apart and start from scratch. We learned a great deal about each other from that project. (Personally, I think she was pleased to see I didn't lose my cool but enjoyed the experience.)

5. When we knew we were definitely going to marry, we went to see a lawyer friend. Barry Vickery was a friend of many years and I knew him to be a man of Christian principles and high integrity. We told him what we were doing and wanted him to help us arrange our possessions and finances with two things in mind: We need to be able to use our assets for the rest of our lives, but to leave them intact so our

children can inherit without too much difficulty. We made several trips to his office before it was all done. There were no serious disagreements. We gave copies of the results to our children.

6. We sought out other mature couples who had married after being widowed. What did you do? How did you decide? What do you wish you had done differently? They were all helpful.

7. Watch for the red flags, anything that frightens you or gives concern to your family members. A pastor's widow told Bertha that she had met a man she liked very much. But as they dated, she began to withdraw from the relationship when he started to pressure her to sell her home and move in with him and put the proceeds from her home into a joint account for their living expenses. Everything about that sounds like a man who is scamming widows.

While I Was Praying for The Lord to Lead Me to A Wife, Bertha Was Writing in Her Journal Why She Would Never Marry Again!

A year after the Lord took Margaret, my son announced they would be moving to Mobile,

Alabama. After a quarter-century in the New Orleans area I would no longer have any family member there. So, that's when I began praying in earnest for the Lord to lead me. People laugh at the prayer I was praying...

"Lord, if you have someone for me, here is what I would like! Intelligent and godly. Sweet and humble. Attractive is good. And Lord, let her not have any complications in her personal life like grown kids who lay around the house goofing off. Marry her and your life becomes about them. And lastly, Lord, whoever she is (I knew it was no one I knew), let us both know it up front, so we won't play games."

Two days after Bertha and I met, I told her what I'd been praying. She said, "Well, I've been writing in my journal 25 reasons why I will never marry again!" We laughed. The big reason, incidentally, was that she had had 52 years married to the greatest guy in the world--Dr. Gary Fagan--so what are the chances of Act 2 to follow that?

Early on, after we began to sense what the Lord was doing in this, Bertha asked, "What would be a deal-breaker for you in this?" My answer will reveal how silly I can be at a serious time. But what I said--and I really said it--was: "Three things. 1. Do you smoke? 2. Were you ever a man? And 3. Do you still work at the road house over on the highway?"

She laughed at my goofy answer. Later, when we began to share this with friends, I suggested that her answer to my questions was: "I can confidently say 'no' to two of those!"

Bertha's daughter Lari sent me a note just a month after we had met. "Thank you for giving my mother her laughter back." We loved that.

I read somewhere that if there is no laughter in your lovemaking, you're doing it all wrong. We have lots of laughter in this household.

A FEW QUESTIONS PEOPLE ASK ON THE SUBJECT OF REMARRYING...

1. *What if your kids are opposed to the marriage?*

Every family is different. No one will know better than you how much weight to give to their opposition. Sometimes, they just need assurance that Mom is acting wisely. A little more time should take care of that. At other times, the kids fear losing their inheritance. That's where the pre-nuptial agreement comes in handy.

2. *What about pre-nuptial agreements? Aren't they for people who intend to divorce?*

Granted, that's how we all hear about them. But when my little sister Susan was widowed and later when she met George Boswell and they decided to marry, they worked out the pre-nup with a lawyer in order to be able to use their assets for living but leave them intact for distribution to heirs after they're in Heaven. So, Susan encouraged us to do the same.

3. Are the legal fees high? Ours was most reasonable. But that depends on the lawyer, I would think. Before choosing a lawyer, ask around. And before hiring one, ask what he will charge for this service.

4. Joe and Bertha, would you post on these pages a copy of your pre-nup as a guide for the rest of us? No, I don't think so. But thanks for asking.

Chapter Eleven

Can We Say A Few Things on The Subject of Dying If We Promise Not to Get Morbid?

William Saroyan, the famous author, said, "Everyone has got to die, but I've always believed an exception would be made in my case." He died in 1981 at the age of 73.

No exceptions. "It is appointed unto man once to die...." (Hebrews 9:27).

When I was diagnosed with cancer in 2004, I remember thinking, "Wait a minute! Other people get cancer. I'm a pastor. I don't get cancer." But I did. That dreaded monster is no respect of persons.

I don't know anything good to say about death except one thing: On the other side, Heaven awaits. Death is like a door; on this side it reads "exit" and on the other, "entrance."

So, we think of death as a valley through which we have to walk. We each have to get through it.

"Try to get through it." I heard Dr. James Dobson give that bit of advice to the mother of a teenager one time. I burst out laughing. It was the last thing I would have expected from this font of wisdom on family life. But it was exactly right.

And so with death. We go through it. But there's good news...

In the 1943 book *Paris Underground,* American housewife Etta Shiber tells how she was caught in Paris when the Germans marched in and took over in June of 1940. She and a friend spent a full year helping downed British flyers get back home until the Nazis discovered what they were doing and arrested them. In 1943 she was exchanged for a German spy and returned home to America. She promptly wrote her story in this fascinating book. One small paragraph was worth the price of the book.

After taking over, the Germans sealed the borders around the portion of France under their control and refused to allow anyone to leave. The citizenry however did all they could to slip out of the Nazi occupation across the lines into what was called "unoccupied France." They found some ingenuous ways to get out of the country. Mrs. Shiber writes,

Many ingenuous ruses were used to cross the line. In one village, for instance, there was a cemetery whose main gate opened into occupied territory. But in the rear wall was an old forgotten door which had not served for years; and that was in unoccupied territory. (Villagers) at first were surprised to note a sudden increase in the number of mourners at local funerals. But they noted also that fewer mourners returned from the cemetery than went to it; and the old-timers recalled the disused door and realized that it was serving once more.

When I first read that, all the bells went off inside. The Holy Spirit was sending an alert: This is what the Lord Jesus did. He opened a gate on the back side of the cemetery.

By His death, burial, and resurrection, the Lord Jesus Christ forever changed the nature of death for us.

We still go to graveyards. We just don't spend any time there. We keep walking right on out the back into the land of the free.

Two or three key scriptures make this point in one way or the other. You might want to make a note of these. They will be on the test...

--"...the grace which was given to us in Christ Jesus before time began but has now been revealed by the appearing of our Savior Jesus Christ, *who has abolished death* and brought life and immortality to light through the gospel...." (2 Timothy 1:9-10). Jesus abolished death? Some translations say He "nullified" it. Either way sounds good to me.

--"Inasmuch as the children have partaken of flesh and blood, He Himself likewise shared in the same, that through death He might *destroy him who had the power of death*, that is, the devil, and *release those who through fear of death were subject to bondage all* their lives" (Hebrews 2:14-15). No more fear of death. Imagine that!

By His death, burial, and resurrection the Lord Jesus abolished death, defeated (or destroyed) the devil and delivered the captives. No wonder we make so much of that first Easter weekend!

No more fear!

The song says, "no guilt in life, no fear in death; This is the power of Christ in me."

One of the most important but hardest lessons for God's people to get through their heads is that Jesus Christ is insulted when His people fear death! Death is defeated, overthrown, and its days are numbered. True, "the last enemy that shall be destroyed is death," according to First Corinthians 15:26.

It helps me to realize Jesus hated death far more than we. He broke up every funeral procession He came to by raising the dead.

The B.C. comic strip, written and drawn by the late (and inimitable) Johnny Hart has the little king asking the priest, "So, you say your Lord descended into hell, is that right?" The priest answers, "Just long enough to pick up the keys." That's great theology and from a comic strip, no less. In Revelation 1, we see the ascended and glorified Lord Jesus Christ saying, "I am He who lives, and was dead, and behold, I am alive forevermore. Amen. And I have the keys of Hades and of Death" (Revelation 1:18).

So, while death remains the mystery of the ages for us, we are not to fear it. We are to go forward in faith, knowing that Jesus Christ is in charge and on the other side is "the Father's house."

A father and son were traveling in the car when suddenly the child began screaming. A honeybee was flying around inside the car. The child was allergic to bee-sting and the family had been told a sting could be fatal. As the child is screaming in fear, the father slows the car down and pulls onto the shoulder of the road. Meanwhile, he reaches out and catches the bee in his hand. Then, he quietens the child, rolls down the windows, and releases the bee. Seeing the bee flying, the child began screaming again. But the father said, "Son, look here. The bee left his stinger in my hand. That's one bee that can't ever bother anyone else." Scripture says, "O death, where is thy sting? Thanks be to God who gives us the victory!" (I Corinthians 15:55,57). Death is still buzzing around scaring people; but if you are in Christ Jesus, it's unable to do you any permanent harm.

In the early days of the American west, wagon trains feared prairie fires more than anything. The sight of a fire on the horizon struck terror into the hearts of the travelers. But eventually, someone had a bright idea. When a fire was spotted in the distance, someone set a back fire and burned off an acre or two. Then, the wagons and livestock were pulled onto the burned over ground. When the fire came, it went around them. That's a little parable for believers. Someday the fires of God's judgment will fall on humanity. All will stand before the Lord and give account. Every eye will see the Lord Jesus and every tongue shall confess that He is Lord. We shall all give account for what we have done in this life. God's judgment will be fearsome. However, there is one place in the universe where His judgment has already fallen: At Calvary. Those who are in Christ will be safe forever.

Ruth Bell Graham used to tell of something that happened in the family of her Presbyterian pastor in Montreat, NC, many years earlier when he was a child. The pastor's father's name was Bob and he had a 16-year-old brother named Robbie. Bob's mother was in a nursing home and he went by to see her every day. One day Robbie came down with some strange life-threatening virus and he was put in ICU in the hospital. Because Bob's mother doted on that wonderful grandson so much, Bob never told her that Robbie was gravely ill. So, now poor Bob was back and forth, ministering to his mother in the nursing home and his son in the hospital. One day, Robbie died. With his heart broken, Bob left the cemetery and drove to the nursing home to check on his mother. The doctor was just leaving her room.

"Your mother has slipped into a coma," he said. "But sit with her and hold her hand and talk with her." For an hour or more Bob sat with his mother who was unresponsive in the coma. Then, suddenly, she opened her eyes. "Why, there's Mama," she said. "And there's Papa. And there's Jesus." And she named some other friends long since gone to Heaven. And then Bob heard her say, "Why there's Robbie. I didn't know Robbie had died. Poor Bob." And she closed her eyes and went to Heaven.

I love that. And have no trouble believing that Robbie was with Jesus. After all, to be absent from the body is to be present with the Lord (2 Corinthians 5).

Some fellow asked his pastor, "When are you preachers going to quit talking about dying?" The minister said, "Just as soon as they quit dying."

Chapter Twelve

Chapter 12

Some Quick Stories About Senior Adults We Know, Have Known, Or Wish We Could Have Known....

Bill Taylor posted a note on Facebook today to announce he was 79. And he seems quite pleased with that! Bill is energetic and youthful, always friendly and happy. You'd love him. Bill--aka "Mister Sunday School" for a full generation of Southern Baptists-- has served some of the great churches of the land in educational and discipleship leadership. This morning, according to his post, he logged 12 miles on his bike. His beautiful wife Rose walked 4 miles. These days, Bill is working with his son Brent and others in a ministry of leadership development called Unlimited Partnerships. Lately they have branched out to Baylor University and Dallas Baptist University. He has no intention of retiring, ever!

Eddie Kinchen is a deacon in our church (Jackson, Mississippi's First Baptist Church). Eddie turned 80 not long ago. He's youthful and active, a greeter at our church and an encourager to everyone. Eddie called recently, asking me to have lunch with him and a college student whom he is mentoring. This Ole Miss student is the president of his fraternity (a huge one and he says they abide by Christian standards!) with plans to head to seminary and pastor a church. Eddie has a dozen or so whom he is mentoring all the time. What exactly does he do? "I pray for them regularly, send them notes of encouragement, and once in a while I'll buy them a book and take them to lunch." He has been known to arrange scholarships for deserving and needy students. He has been called "the ultimate Barnabas."

Doug Dillard was the first cartoonist to make it big in the Southern Baptist Convention. His "Brother Blotz" and "Pulpitears" were all the rage when I was a young pastor in Christian publications and volumes of cartoons. Doug is still with us, I'm happy to say. Here's what he said on his Facebook page today: "At

89, I have other things (than cartooning) on which to spend my time: living here in what I call 'the vestibule of heaven' with my childhood sweetheart, who needs me now more than ever. We are acting our age, you might say, enjoying it immensely, confident that when we had our turn at bat, we did our best to swing for the fences. Now it is time to take a walk."

Dottie Hudson is a member of our church. She's in her 80s, and a member of our church's pastor search committee. Last year, she wrote a biography of her father, Dr. Roland Q. Leavell, who was for many years President of our New Orleans Baptist Theological Seminary. Dottie returned to LSU when she was 50 to get a degree in counseling. Not long ago, when she was nearing her 80th birthday, our church honored her as she officially retired from our family counseling ministry. Dottie says, however, her favorite role was pastor's wife. Her man, Dr. Carl Hudson, has been with the Lord some years now.

Bobby and Joyce Covington of Macon, Georgia, are longtime friends of Bertha and Gary, all the way back to 1966 when Gary began directing Youth for Christ here in Jackson. They actively supported this ministry through money, prayer, and counsel. They've worked in Gideons, taken mission trips to Malawi, Brazil, and other countries, all while faithfully serving in their churches. Now in their late 80s, we had a visit with them just this week. They look beautiful and are still active for the Lord. Bobby does a weekly Bible study at a local prison, and they host a neighborhood Bible study in their home each week.

Dick and Charlotte Day. Only a few days ago, we learned of the death of one of our dear friends, Dick Day. Dick and his wife Charlotte had ministered in Malawi, Africa, for 25 years. Our daughter Lari sent an Instagram photo of Dick's gravesite. The caption over the photo read:

"My dear friend Charlotte Day laying a wreath on the grave of her husband Dick in the graveyard where the chiefs are buried in Makungula Village in Malawi. This is where Charlotte began the first preschool and Gogo group. Over 500 came to say goodbye, from the American Ambassador to former

students, old Gogos (grandmothers who take care of orphaned children), children, and chiefs. The Chief spoke and said that for children yet unborn, they will ask why this American was buried in their village, and they will be told of Dick and Charlotte's love for Jesus and for the people of Malawi."

Billy and Mary Jane Primos. Friends in the Jackson, Mississippi area will know this name! Primos restaurants are all over the metro area. Over 45 years ago when I was living in this city the first time and on staff at First Baptist Church, Primos restaurant was across the street from the church. Everyone knew Billy and Mary Jane. Well, these days, their children and grandchildren have the business and, as I say, they've multiplied the locations. But every Sunday we see Billy and Mary Jane at church. They're smiling, greeting people, and being the same loving, charming friends they've always been. To my question, Billy said he was 84 and Mary Jane a year younger. "But I'm younger than my siblings," he said, "and all are still going strong!"

Joel Davis of Atlanta. Joel was my roommate during college and was used of the Lord to help me during some pivotal moments. He was best man in our 1962 wedding. These days, Joel is in his mid-80s and living the life. Last year, he retired from Annistown Road Baptist Church (which he helped a pastor friend plant more than 25 years back!) as their senior adult minister. Joel is a constant witness for the Lord and a prayer warrior. I'll never forget the time, maybe 40 years ago, when he and I brought our four sons and met up at an Atlanta Braves ballgame. At one point, he said, "Wilma and I pray for you every day." Now, mind you, we saw each other maybe once a decade. That kind of faithfulness is a treasure beyond compare.

Fred McFeely Rogers (1928-2003)

This amazing man who influenced two generations of children wrote this: "Each generation in its turn is a link between all that has gone before and all that comes after. This is true genetically, and it is equally true in the transmission of identity. Our parents gave us what they were able to give, and we took what we could of it and made it part of ourselves. If we knew our grandparents, and even great-grandparents, we will have taken from them what they could offer us, too. All that helped to make us who we are. We, in our turn, will offer what we can of ourselves to our children and their offspring."

He said, "I do love being a grandfather, and I wonder if it wasn't because my grandfather McFeely loved me so much, and I had such a good time with him."

It was Grandfather Fred McFeely who would say to young Freddie at the conclusion of his visits to the farm, "I like you just the way you are." Fred conveyed the same message to millions of little children through his television program "Mister Rogers' Neighborhood." The influence of his grandfather goes forward!

Joe's dad, Carl J. McKeever (1912-2007)

Dad was 90 years old when he walked into our hotel room in Montgomery, Alabama. Later that morning I was to address a statewide luncheon involving the governor, legislature, state Supreme Court, and leading pastors from around the state. My hosts had okayed my request to have my father present. The night before, older brother Ron had spent the night at the family farmhouse. Then, leaving very early the next morning, he and Dad made the 160-mile drive, arriving around 10 am. As they entered our room, my wife Margaret gave Dad a hug and said, "How are you feeling, Pop?" That's when my wonderful dad uttered a line for the ages. He said, "Well, when I got up this morning, I decided not to ask myself that question because I might not like the answer!"

Joe's mother, Lois Kilgore McKeever (1916-2012)

On a similar vein, when my Mom was 90--and a widow by then--one of the grand- or great-grandchildren would spend the night with her in the farmhouse. Each morning, I'd give her a call from my home or car (I lived 400 miles away). One Sunday morning, on my way somewhere to preach, I called her. She said, "Jon spent the night with me. At breakfast I said, 'Jon, are you going to church?' He said, 'Aw Granny, I don't feel like it.' I told him 'Oh, honey--if I only went to church when I felt like it, I'd never go.'"

Bertha's mother, Laura Overby Pepper (1913-1998)

During the last five years of her life, Mother lived in a nursing home. Even with dementia, she always knew her room number (27), always remembered daughter Laura's name, and could recite the alphabet backwards. "Mother always wanted to write a book. A high school teacher had told her she needed to write a book someday. Mother wrote that book with her life." Bertha and Laura say, "I hope I finish as well."

Daniel Auber, French composer (1782-1871)

A friend greeted Auber at the opera and said, "We're getting older, aren't we?" Auber sighed, "Well, there's no help for it. Aging seems to be the only available way to live a long time."

Auber refused to think about death and therefore would not talk about it. However, when attending a funeral service, he couldn't get out of, he remarked to a fellow mourner, "I believe this is the last time I'll take part as an amateur."

Cato (234-149 BC) Roman statesman

When Cato was 80, he began studying Greek. When asked why he took upon himself such a task at his advanced age, he replied that it was the youngest age he had left.

Winston Churchill (1874-1965) British Statesman

When the great Prime Minister was 80, the photographer who was taking his picture said he hoped he could photograph him on his one-hundredth. "I don't see why not, young man," said Churchill. "You look reasonably fit to me."

One day, in his eighties, Churchill paid a visit to the House of Commons. His sudden appearance created a scene and drew attention from the debate on the floor. An MP said irritably, "After all, they say he's potty." Churchill said, "Yes, and they say he can't hear either."

Ralph Waldo Emerson (1803-1882) Writer, philosopher

In his later years, Emerson's memory grew worse and worse. When he could not think of the word for something, he would "have to refer to them in a circumlocutory way, saying, for instance 'the implement that cultivates the soil,' for plow." Worse, he forgot people's names. At Longfellow's funeral, he said, "That gentleman has a sweet, beautiful soul, but I have entirely forgotten his name." He called an umbrella "the thing that strangers take away."

And my favorite senior in Scripture, Barzillai (11th century B.C.)

A lesser known octogenarian in Scripture is Barzillai, from 2 Samuel 19. When David's son Absalom was leading a rebellion and trying to take over the kingdom, the royal family fled Jerusalem. As they crossed the Jordan, three wealthy landowners hosted the sizeable group. Sometime later, after Absalom was dead and the insurrection had fizzled out, David brings his people back down to the Jordan for the return trip to Jerusalem. They pause there, and David turns to Barzillai, his primary host for these weeks. He says, "Come go home with me and I'll return your wonderful hospitality."

The old gentleman said, "I am eighty years old, sir. I can't taste food any more. I can't hear singing. I'd just be a burden to you." And then, suddenly, he had an idea. Turning to one of his sons, Barzillai said, "But here is Chimham. Take him and do for him whatever you would have done for me." Just that quickly was Chimham's life changed forever! There is evidence that David gave Chimham part of his personal estate in Bethlehem. Four hundred years later, when travelers were heading from Jerusalem to Egypt and would pass by Bethlehem, it was said "they stayed at the lodge of Chimham" (Jeremiah 41:17). Think of it--Chimham's descendants were still living there.

Wouldn't it be great to do something for a child today to change his/her destiny forever? So, Barzillai is one of our great champions in Scripture, an old man getting it right.

Larry Black, longtime minister of music for Southern Baptists

For over 30 years, Larry Black served the great First Baptist Church of Jackson MS (our home church) as minister of music. He built one of the greatest music programs ever, and was always in demand to work with great preachers and evangelists in crusades. These days, Larry is retired and living near us. He performed our wedding in January of 2017 and is a dear friend. In his retirement, Larry is constantly helping churches with their choirs and music programs.

Larry has a foundation to assist deserving seminary students and is one of the most energetic and Spirit-filled seniors we know.

Chapter Thirteen

Bertha Gets the Last Word....

Nothing is going to bring back our youth.

Though I am told by my doctor that I am very healthy for my age, *nothing* is going to make me look "young" again! All of these show my age: wrinkles and age spots, loss of muscle, greying hair, some hearing loss, cataract surgeries, new prescription glasses, a slower metabolism so that I cannot eat all of what I love, and less energy. I'm sure there are more signs of aging coming. When our family moved from the deep South to Rhode Island where everything was unlike anything I had ever known, soon the harsh winter set in and I began noticing my dry skin was beginning to wrinkle. I drove across town to a very nice department store with a great line of cosmetics. I asked the cosmetologist, "What can I do for my dry skin? We have just moved from the South, and these are such harsh cold winters." After considering a number of options, she whispered, "Honey, I could sell you many expensive products, but they would fail. You have been programmed from birth to have your mother's skin. Just keep being kind and gentle to your skin and use sunscreen."

This was a bit disconcerting, but she had given me wise and loving advice for a lifetime. Her advice that day may have cost her a sale but guess who I went back to when I needed just regular kinds of cosmetics.

Not everyone is receptive to our knowledge and wisdom.

When I was a young high school English teacher in an inner-city school, I learned that not every student wants to learn, some of whom enjoyed bringing havoc into a classroom. A wise fellow teacher shared with me that when we become angry with children, it uses up all the energy that we need for the day. Why let that happen! Their actions were not worth the detriment to me. This still carries with me today.

Naps are such a good idea!

Many of the world's cultures accept them as part of life. Before full-time retirement, there was not time for them in my life. However, now I relish having a guilt-free nap every day when this is possible. When my first child was born, I was thirty-years-old and had taught high school up until her birth. I was so used to trying to do every little thing, squeezing household duties into every available minute that I began using the time when my daughter was sleeping to accomplish these tasks. However, my wise mother told me how important it was to take a nap in the afternoon, at least part of the time, when my daughter napped. I did work at it. Now that I am usually home in the early afternoon, my husband and I both take a nap and enjoy that we can.

Our goal is to fulfill God's purpose for us in life:

Once when I was walking my little dog up to the post office at the end of our neighborhood in order to mail a letter, it was becoming hotter as we walked the several blocks. On the way back, I could hardly wait to reach home and the air conditioning. I picked up my little Sheltie and walked a little faster until I saw the beautiful older tree whose branches extended over the sidewalk--shade at last! I stopped under the canopy and was refreshed for a few minutes. As I stood there, Psalm 1 entered my mind:

"Oh, the joys of those who delight in doing everything God wants them to, and day and night are always meditating on His laws and thinking about ways to follow Him more closely. They are like trees along a river bank, bearing luscious fruit each season without fail. Their leaves shall never wither, and all they do shall prosper."

In my Bible's margin, I wrote, "The tree each year casts a wider circle and is taller toward the sky and more fruit is borne."

"You are the world's seasoning, to make it tolerable. If you lose your flavor, what will happen to the world? . . .You are the world's light--a city on a hill, glowing in the night for all to see. Don't hide your light! Let it shine for all; let your good deeds glow for all to see, so that they will praise your heavenly Father" (Matthew 5:13-16). This does not specify only the young: it applies to all of us, whatever our age.

How we are seen by others is not all that we are.

We are a combination of all the years of our past: all the acquaintances we have known and been touched by; all the experiences we have had; the places we have lived, the homes that have housed us; all the places where we have traveled; the churches we have been a part of; the paid jobs we have had; the volunteer jobs we have filled; the children and grandchildren that the Lord has given us; all the friends that have meant so much to us; the accumulation of all the knowledge and wisdom that has been passed on to us; and, most of all, our decision to give our lives to the Lord, accepting Jesus Christ's death for us, and all the years of letting Him work in our lives.

We visited a friend and faithful church member sometime after he had been released from his job, which was his and his family's livelihood because of a medical condition that would prevent him from driving. He told us, "This is not who I am; I am a combination of all I have ever been."

We don't have anything to prove except to "finish well."

Most of us still haven't succeeded in applying all to our lives, but like Paul, we do want to finish well. "Dear brothers, I am still not all I should be but I am bringing all my energies to bear on this one thing: Forgetting the past and looking forward to what lies ahead, I strain to reach the end of the race and receive the prize for which God is calling us up to heaven because of what Christ Jesus did for us" (Philippians 3:13,14).

The Lord always fulfils His promises to us.

What a mainstay Lamentations 3:23 has been, "Great is His faithfulness; His loving kindness begins afresh each day." The hymn "Great is Thy Faithfulness" has been the favorite of many of my friends.

Thomas Chisholm was born in a log cabin in Franklin, Kentucky. He became a Christian when he was twenty-seven and entered the ministry nine years later. Poor health forced him to retire after just one year. For the rest of his life, Chisholm lived in New Jersey working as a life insurance agent. He wrote nearly 1,200 poems, with some of them made into hymns.

Chisholm said, "My income has not been large at any time due to impaired health in the earlier years which has followed me on until now. Although I must not fail to record here the unfailing faithfulness of a covenant-keeping God and that He has given me many wonderful displays of His providing care, for which I am filled with astonishing gratefulness."

"Great Is Thy Faithfulness"
by Thomas Chisholm – 1925

Great Is Thy faithfulness, O God my Father!
There is no shadow of turning with Thee;
Though changest not, Thy compassions, they fail not
As Thou hast been Thou forever wilt be.

Refrain:

Great Is Thy faithfulness,
Great Is Thy faithfulness,

Morning by morning new mercies I see;
All I have needed Thy hand hath provided
Great is Thy Faithfulness, Lord unto me!

Summer and winter, and springtime and harvest,
Sun, moon, and stars in their courses above,
Join with all nature in manifold witness
To Thy great faithfulness, mercy, and love.

Refrain
Pardon for Sin and a peace that endureth,
Thine own dear presence to cheer and to guide,
Strength for today and bright hope for tomorrow
Blessings all mine, with ten thousand beside!

Our future is settled and perfect in Heaven.

"Let not your heart be troubled. You are trusting God, now trust in me. 2,3 There are many homes up there where my Father lives, and I am going to prepare them for your coming. When everything is ready, then I will come and get you, so that you can always be with me where I am. If this weren't so, I

would tell you plainly. 4 And you know where I am going and how to get there" **(John 14:2-4).**

When we lived in Brasilia, Brazil, there was a very large area named the Area of *Mansoes* or Area of Mansions. The walls of stone and stucco were very tall so that passersby could not see into the area. The gate would open only to those who were residents. Very beautiful, I'm sure, and only for the rich.

When we die and leave this earthly plane, we will find there are "mansions" *already prepared for us who have repented of our sin and trusted Jesus Christ as our Savior.* John, the writer of **Revelation 21 and 22** was given this to write for us to reveal all we need to know about the city until we view it ourselves. *"Then I saw a new earth and a new sky, for the present earth and sky had disappeared. 2 And I, John, saw the Holy City, the new Jerusalem, coming down from God out of heaven. It was a glorious sight, beautiful as a bride at her wedding. 3 I heard a loud shout from the throne saying, 'Look, the home of God is now among men, and He will live with them and they will be His people; yes, God himself will be among them. 4 He will wipe away all tears from their eyes, and there shall be no more* *death, nor sorrow, nor crying, nor pain. All of that has gone forever.'"*

10 "In a vision He took me to a towering mountain peak and from there I watched that wondrous city, the holy Jerusalem, descending out of the skies from God.

11 It was filled with the glory of God, and flashed and glowed like a precious gem, crystal clear like jasper.

12 Its walls were broad and high, with twelve gates guarded by twelve angels.

13 There were three gates on each side--north, south, east and west.

14 The walls had twelve foundation stones, and on them were written the names of the twelve apostles of the Lamb.

15 The angel held in his hand a golden measuring stick to measure the city and its gates and walls.

16 When he measured it, he found it was a square as wide as it was long; in fact, it was in the form of a cube, for its height was exactly the same as its other dimensions--1500 miles each way. 17 Then he measured the thickness of the walls and found them to be 216 feet across (the angel called out these measurements to me, using standard units).

18,19,20 The city itself was pure, transparent gold like glass! The wall was made of jasper, and was built on twelve layers of foundation stones inlaid with gems: The first layer with jasper; the second with sapphire; the third with chalcedony; the fourth with emerald; the fifth with sardonyx; the sixth layer with sardus; the seventh with chrysolite; the eighth with beryl; the ninth with topaz; the tenth with chrysoprase; the eleventh with jacinth; the twelfth with amethyst.

21 The twelve gates were made of pearls--each gate from a single pearl! And the main street was pure, transparent gold, like glass.

22 No temple could be seen in the city, for the Lord God Almighty and the Lamb are worshiped in it everywhere.

23 And the city has no need of sun or moon to light it, for the glory of God and the Lamb illuminate it.

24 Its light will light the nations of the earth, and the rulers of the world will come and bring their glory to it.

25 Its gates never close; they stay open all day long--and there is no night!

26 And the glory and honor of all nations shall be brought into it.

27 Nothing evil will be permitted in it--no one immoral or dishonest--but only those whose names are written in the Lamb's Book of Life."

Revelation 22 -

1 "And He pointed out to me a river of pure Water of Life, clear as crystal, flowing from the throne of God and the Lamb,

2 coursing down the center of the main street. On each side of the river grew Trees of Life, bearing twelve crops of fruit, with a fresh crop each month; the leaves were used for medicine to heal the nations.

3 There shall be nothing in the city which is evil; for the throne of God and of the Lamb will be there, and His servants will worship Him.

4 And they shall see His face; and His name shall be written on their foreheads.

5 And there will be no night there--no need for lamps or sun-- for the Lord God will be their light; and they shall reign forever and ever.

6,7 Then the angel said to me, 'These words are trustworthy and true: 'I am coming soon! God, who tells His prophets what the future holds, has sent His angel to tell you this will happen soon. Blessed are those who believe it and all else written in the scroll"(**LVB**).

About the Authors....

JOE MCKEEVER is a native of Nauvoo, Alabama and the son of a coal miner. He grew up on an Alabama farm and in a West Virginia mining camp. Joe has degrees from Birmingham-Southern College (A.B. in history) and New Orleans Baptist Theological Seminary (masters and doctorate). The last churches he pastored were FBC of Columbus, MS, FBC Charlotte, NC, and FBC Kenner, LA. He served as Director of Missions for the New Orleans Baptist Association from 2004 to 2009. He was DOM there when Katrina went through in '05 (which accounts for the white hair, he says). Joe's wife of 52 years Margaret Henderson died in January of 2015. He and Bertha Fagan met 13 months later and married a year after that. Joe and Margaret have 3 children and 8 grandchildren. Joe is a sketch artist (for churches, conventions, weddings, etc.), a blogger at www.joemckeever.com and a cartoonist for Baptist Press (see www.bpnews.net). He is the author of *Help! I'm a Deacon!* and co-author with Bertha of *Grief Recovery 101.* They live in Ridgeland, MS, a suburb of Jackson.

BERTHA FAGAN MCKEEVER is a native of Jackson, Mississippi. After graduating from Forest Hill High School (where she was homecoming queen), she earned a bachelor's degree from Bob Jones University and later a masters from Rhode Island College. She is a lifelong teacher, whether in high school or college or online. Presently, she is on the adjunct faculty for Hinds Community College and teaches online for Taylor University of Indiana. Bertha was married to Dr. Gary Fagan for 52 years before the Lord took him in May of 2014. They served churches in Alabama, Massachusetts, Florida, and Mississippi, and as missionaries to Malawi and Brazil. Gary directed Youth for Christ in Jackson and in Atlanta. Bertha and Gary had two children, Lari and Jeff, and six grandchildren. Bertha is co-author with Joe of *Grief Recovery 101*. They live in Ridgeland, MS, just north of Jackson, in a lovely little neighborhood, with a pond in their back yard.

CPSIA information can be obtained
at www.ICGtesting.com
Printed in the USA
FFHW01n2223211018
48873863-53085FF

9 781946 478924